And the Pink Snow fell...

The Story of the Port Hope Gas Explosion

Dave & Marguerite,

Thanks for standing with us and being such good friends.

Ray Cross
February 20, 1996

Essence
PUBLISHING

Belleville, Ontario, Canada

And the **Pink Snow** *fell...*

ISBN: 1-896400-03-5

Essence Publishing
103B Cannifton Road,
Belleville, ON K8N 4V2

Printed in Canada

◆ STRATHROSE ESTATES ◆

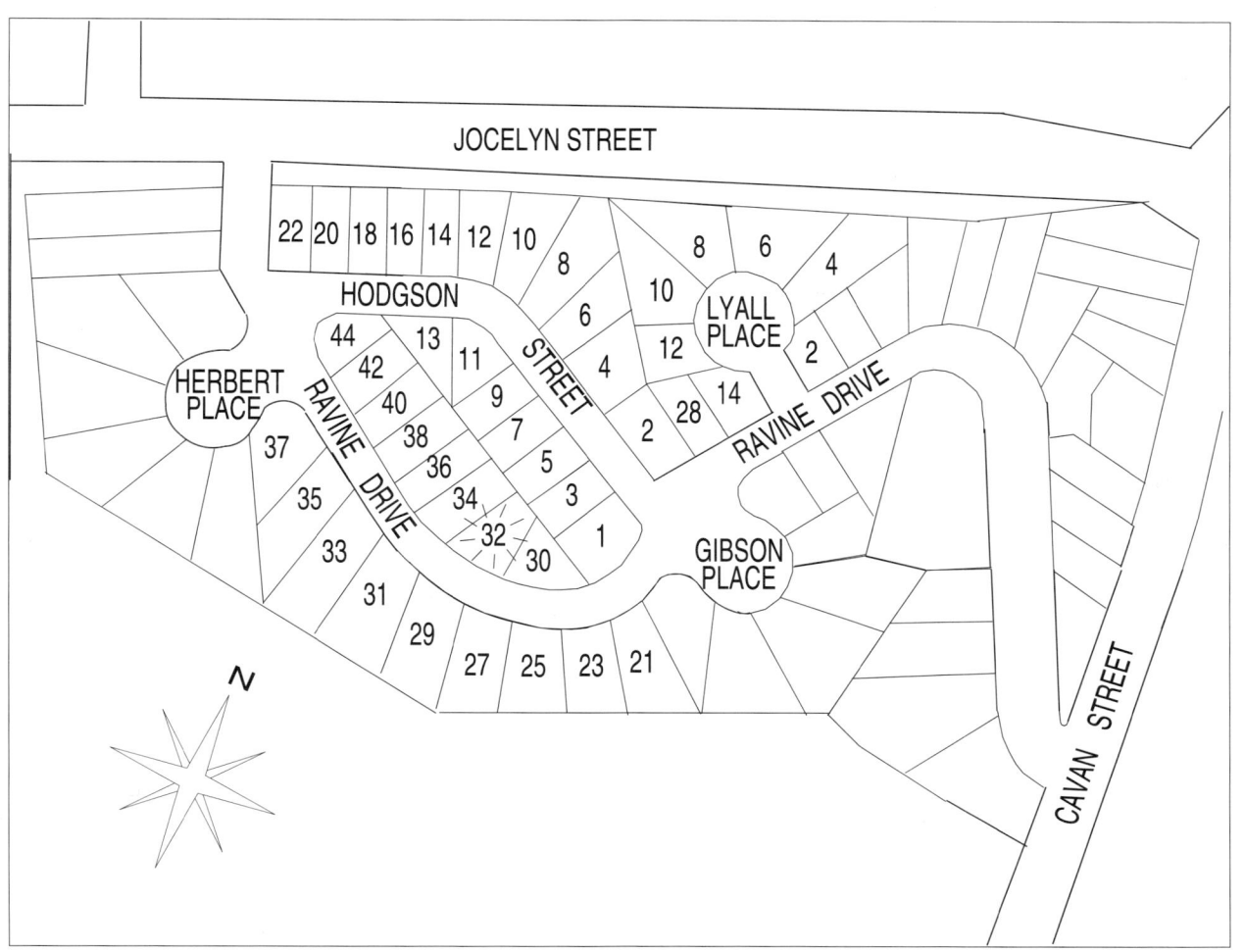

The Floor plan of 30 Ravine Drive and 32 Ravine Drive.

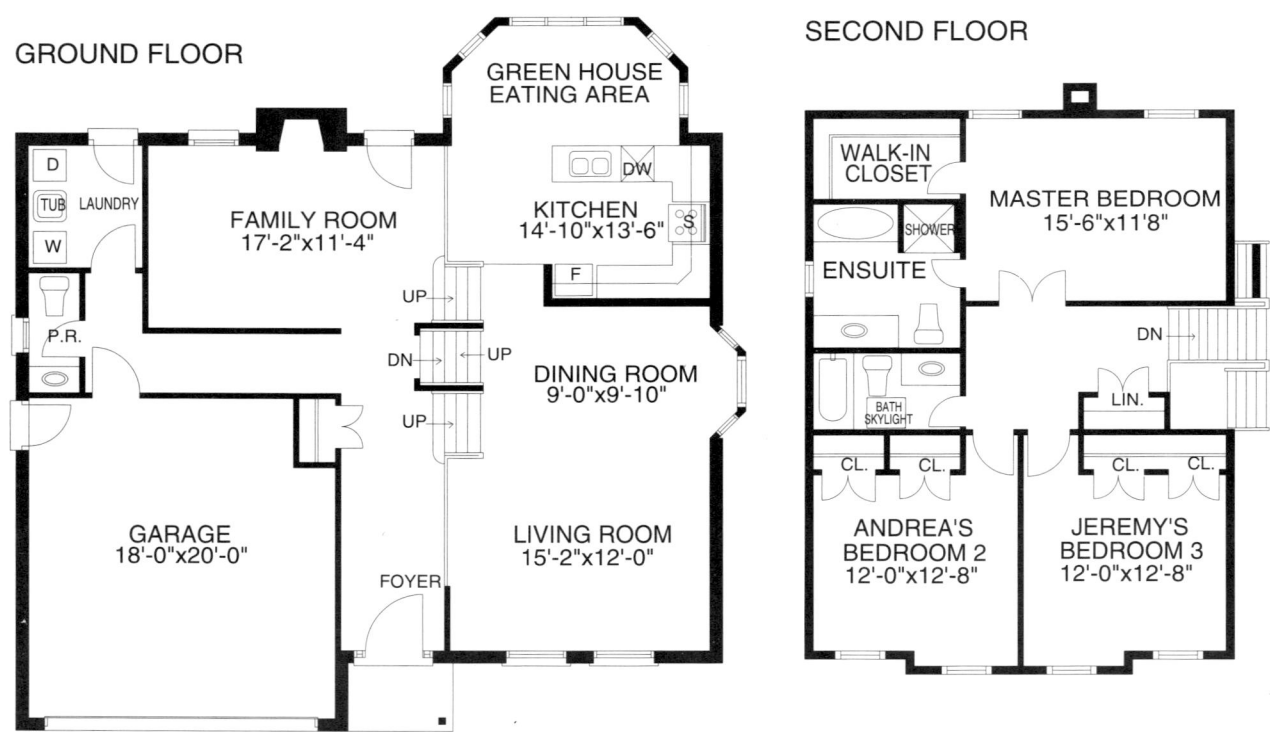

Both homes were Westchesters by Halminen Homes Inc.,
except that 32 Ravine Drive had a triple car rather than
a double car garage.

The explosion invaded 30 Ravine Drive from the west,
i.e., from left to right.

CONTENTS

❄

A Rumbling Rumour
The Gas is Coming
A Bewildered Family

A Monster Breathed
Our Home Crumpled
Day of Contrasts
And the Fires Raged
Our Home Targeted
Expansion and Co-existence
Walls Sucked and Suspended
Cabinets Unravelled
And the Pink Snow Fell

"I was there!"
A Two Stage Explosion
The Strathrose Regatta

"I Almost Lost Mine"
Wide Eyed Across the Street
A Vine Cut Off

FOREWORD

Suddenly the lives of dozens of people changed on the morning of November 10, 1993, in a quiet subdivision in Port Hope, Ontario.

A house had been blown sky high in a gas explosion.

Miraculously, no one was physically injured.

People wandered about the explosion site awestruck by what they saw.

Rev. Cross and his wife, Diane, were among the victims of the explosion that morning. Their home, on a lot adjacent to the explosion site, suffered severe damage and was eventually condemned.

Without a home or possessions, numbed by what had happened to them and trying to help their children cope with the loss, the Crosses persevered.

Rev. Cross had ministered to families and individuals for many years before he and his family were faced with the loss of their home and an uncertain future.

As he had so often counselled others to do who were trying to cope with life-changing trauma, Rev. Cross wrote down what was happening to them and how they were reacting to the stress.

In his book, *And the Pink Snow Fell...*, he provides a living example of how a family copes with the tragedies of life.

Imagine having your house literally cave in around you as you sit with your spouse in bed enjoying a cup of tea.

The Cross family continues to recover from their heartache, losses, both financial and personal, and from the assault on their psyches.

The front page national and international news coverage brought the story of the Port Hope house explosion into the homes of millions of people. But as so often happens, the inside stories are the ones seldom told.

In sharing his memories of the life-changing event in his own words, Rev. Cross offers lessons to us all on how to cope when it seems we are alone against the world.

Peggy Foster
Staff Reporter
Port Hope Evening Guide

ACKNOWLEDGEMENTS

❄

I owe a debt of thanks to a number of people who shared their experiences, assistance and advice to bring this project to print:

My son, Jeremy, Doug Buchan and Dieter Marschke who enabled the digital transfer of videos to still frames.

Rick Gibson, whose computer drafting skills provided the subdivision map and floor plans.

Port Hope Evening Guide reporter, Peggy Foster, who offered invaluable advice and encouragement.

All of those whose experiences added such depth to my understanding of that fateful day.

Friends and family who read the manuscript at various stages and offered suggestions.

To the best of my ability, I have verified all facts from primary sources and accurately reported all opinions expressed in this book. I sincerely believe it captures the true event and stories surrounding it.

CHAPTER ONE

BUILDING UP TO THE EXPLOSION

In my mind,
Wednesday, November 10, 1993 is forever etched
as the day time stood still
and
the pink snow fell.

A RUMBLING RUMOUR

The sun glowed brightly the morning of November 10, 1993, as a helicopter from *CHCH-TV Hamilton* rose skyward. Like a soap bubble, it floated eastward along the north shore of Lake Ontario. Beneath it, a million stories were unfolding as Toronto yawned, stretched and put on its work clothes. But that day Toronto's stories would wait. That day's destination was an early competitor for the name "Toronto" — the historic hamlet of Port Hope.

Nestled into the contours of the Ganaraska River valley, Port Hope is renowned as a pleasant and picturesque place to settle and raise a family. Known originally as Smith's Creek, the Town of Port Hope was officially incorporated in 1834. Steeped in history, it has been a mill town, a port, a brewing centre. In bygone years, it tanned leather and created fashionable horse drawn carriages. Through the years, famous residents have called Port Hope home: Joseph Scriven, writer of the popular hymn, "What a Friend We Have in Jesus," and the Great Farini, who, like Blondin, walked tight ropes over the Niagara Gorge. Among others of note, author Farley Mowat and artist David Blackwood reside in its historical homes.

Port Hope is a town of heritage and culture, but this morning none of this mattered to those approaching from the south. A rumbling rumour had captured the air waves — a catastrophic story reminiscent of wartime memories. Though everywhere else seemed normal, on a hilltop, in a four-year old subdivision in this quiet country town, devastation had been unleashed.

As the helicopter approached and hovered in the sky, lives unravelled amid the rubble on the ground. Like a hummingbird, the "chopper" descended upon the vacant lot at 11 and 13 Hodgson Street to disgorge its cargo of reporters. Video cams, cameras, tape recorders and note pads gathered data for sculpting into newscasts and articles for *The Toronto Star*, *The Toronto Sun*, *The Port Hope Evening Guide*, *The Cobourg Daily Star*, *The Northumberland News*, *Cobourg's CHUC-Radio*, *CHEX-TV Peterborough*, *CFTO-TV* and *CHCH-TV Hamilton*. National news casts highlighted the story, major newspapers across the country gave it front page billing and wire services carried it continent wide. Even the *National Examiner*, with editorial offices in Boca Raton, Florida, published a picture and brief article of the event.

The debris field on Ravine Drive, as viewed from the CHCH-TV helicopter.

Since reporters from all news services focused primarily on 32 Ravine Drive and its residents, many stories were never told. This is one of those stories — the story of the Port Hope explosion and its consequences from the view point of the Cross family of 30 Ravine Drive: Reverend Ray Cross, his wife Diane, and

The Cross family of 30 Ravine Drive: Jeremy and Andrea, Diane and Ray.

children, Jeremy (age 20) and Andrea (age 17). The severe damage to 30 Ravine Drive so graphically demonstrated the ferocity of the fireball that photographers often framed it as the backdrop in published pictures of the aftermath. Furthermore, while thankfully 32 Ravine Drive was unoccupied when it disintegrated, in that fateful moment, Ray and Diane were in the end of their house closest to 32 Ravine Drive. Though sitting merely ten metres away from the explosion, and having their home fold in around them, they walked away from the holocaust unscathed — physically.

THE GAS IS COMING

"The gas is coming! The gas is coming!" The refrain reverberated through Strathrose Estates during the summer of 1993. Home owners on the hill eagerly anticipated the arrival of the pipeline because electric furnaces punched holes in budgets. For our part, we never noticed. Burning wood in our air-tight insert almost completely heated our open-concept home. We did not plan to convert to gas. To us it was an extra expense of little benefit.

Construction began during the summer as crews installed a main gas line to and through Strathrose Estates. Painstakingly, they fished orange pipe through augured tunnels, then filled the access holes. Contractors vied for permission to hook each household to the system. Fluorescent paint on lawns marked conduit routes. Trenching followed, then meters, then heat. It was all so routine.

Due to the possibility of explosion, Vivian MacDonald was fearful of having gas piped into her recently purchased home, but projected savings in heating costs and reassurances that her fears were unfounded ruled the day. So our neighbours, Scott Plummer and Vivian MacDonald, contracted a local firm, Watson's Heating, to install and hook up a gas furnace and water heater. It was an all-day job. At eight o'clock in the evening, November 9, all connections were complete and tested, and approval was granted to open the valve.

But something was wrong. An unusual acrid odour hung in the air. Within an hour of the crew's departure, Scott phoned the installer to express concern. Because he considered the sulphurous smell normal from new equipment, Bill Watson chose to defer inspection until the next day. He told Scott not to worry; it was only the residue burning off; the smell would go away soon. But it didn't.

So..., as the nauseating fumes intensified, the Plummers opened their windows. Scott and the boys, Matthew (age 2) and Marc (age 13), went to bed, but Vivian stayed up to prepare for her next day's teaching of grade eight at Dr. Hawkins School. Since it was mid-November, she began to feel chilly as she worked. She closed windows on the main floor and then retired also.

Gene Szabo, an inspector with the Ontario Fire Marshal's Office, reported that keeping windows open in the basement and bedrooms probably saved their lives. Letting outside air in kept the gas and air mixture below the explosive range. But, had Vivian shut the basement windows instead of those on the main floor, the house would have probably blown during the night, killing or maiming all inside.

As it was, they spent a fitful night, and Vivian, who was four months pregnant, woke with a sore throat and an awful feeling in the pit of her stomach. Even in the morning the fumes persisted, so Scott called the installer again. Mr. Watson promised to come by to check it out with the gas company shortly.

Since it was his scheduled day off from the family business, Plummer's Pharmacy, Scott anticipated being home with his son that November 10. But, because his father was recuperating from surgery, he was called in to work. Had he remained home, windows would have been left open and the explosion averted, but duty called. Windows were shut. The door was locked. Another domino toward destruction was set in place.

Ten metres to the east, my wife, Diane, and I slept soundly through the night, knowing nothing of events next door. For us, Wednesday, November 10 began slowly and peacefully....

At 32 Ravine Drive, methane seeped into the basement and slithered up stair wells. Floor by floor it crept until all five side-split levels reeked. Steadily it percolated into every cavity: infiltrating every room and the garage, invading cabinets, impregnating closets, towels and linens, saturating insulation, mixing a mighty oxygenated molotov cocktail. The servicemen were delayed — an appointment miles away in Cobourg took precedence.

Before 9:00 a.m., Heather Sculthorpe smelled gas as she left her home across the street for work. As soon as she arrived downtown at the Big Brothers office where she works, she reported her concerns to Centra Gas.

At the east wall of 34 Ravine Drive that morning, a serviceman checking a recent fireplace installation to the Novinka's home heard the curious sound of the gas meter whirring at 32 Ravine Drive. Though unrelated to his task, after returning to home base, he reported the anomaly.

Slowly, insidiously, the sinister spirits of doom sought excitement. A door bell, any appliance would do. A timer, a click, an insignificant spark. Based on the fact that Vivian MacDonald had set the dishwasher to begin its cycle at approximately the time of the explosion, it is believed a spark from a switch in that appliance ignited the fumes that shattered the scenic subdivision that looks over the church spires and everyday world of Port Hope.

In a split second, a place designed and decorated for family, for entertainment, for rest and relaxation, became a bomb. Every molecule of air ignited instantaneously and expanded astronomically. It clawed for open windows or cracks to escape, but there were none sufficient....

A BEWILDERED FAMILY

The Cross family had owned the home next door to 32 Ravine Drive for more than two years. I had brought my family to the community to pastor The First Baptist Church of Port Hope. My service to that congregation had ended abruptly, leaving me unemployed for ten months. In December 1992, I began pastoring Harmony Road Baptist Church in Oshawa. Since effective pastoring requires that the minister be resident in the community he serves, our home had been on the real estate market for some time. But things were slow. Real estate professionals were unable to find a buyer so I proceeded to market the home myself. After several months, I succeeded in selling the home to buyers moving to Ontario from Vancouver. But since negotiations for our purchase of a home in Oshawa fell through again and again, we arranged a flexible closing date. November 10, 1993, brought us within ten days of the final date of closing — with no place to go. It was the type of bewildering circumstance one never anticipates facing.

Since I'd be busy late into the evening that November 10, I took the morning to spend time with my wife, Diane. I made tea and we sat in bed discussing plans for our future move. It was one of those simple moments of delight based on oneness of spirit.

CHAPTER TWO

THE EXPLOSION LETS LOOSE

A MONSTER BREATHED

Then a horrific rumbling tore the air. Windows on both sides blasted into our bedroom unleashing a sand storm of debris. Then, as though apologizing for the intrusion, it turned around and ran out, only to return again and again until the gale subsided. Though occupying only a few seconds, the picture frames moved slowly through the shutter of my mind giving the sense of slow motion sustained images. I remember wondering how strange that our intruders did not stay, and that they were capable of such abrupt changes in direction.

I counted four successive invasions and retreats, as though something immense were breathing. Later, I assessed and confirmed such rapid expansion of gases creates a vacuum at the centre. The explosion, therefore, reaches out then recoils, bashing into itself, only to lurch outward and repeat the cycle again and again, producing successive waves of explosion-implosion until the energy released exhausts itself.

While smaller particles rhythmically pulsated in and out of our room, as Diane screamed, larger pieces danced outward like a great chorus line. They had too much explosive momentum to be influenced by the weaker force of implosion. They had been launched like huge pellets from a supercharged cannon. Laws of nature seemed suspended. Gravity hid itself and wind resistance took a hike, while objects not made for flight careened recklessly toward adjoining yards and houses. To my mind, they resembled the blur of near objects from the window of a speeding car or the blasting of droplets from a high pressure hose, but Diane, whose attention throughout the explosion was focused out the window, saw chunks of house rolling in the wind.

In a radius surrounding 32 Ravine Drive, windows exploded, pictures dropped, garage doors buckled, roofs lifted, trusses twisted, siding blew away, aluminum soffits popped, brick walls buckled, foundations and basement floors cracked. Immediately to the west, at 34 Ravine Drive, besides internal structural damage, the roof was lifted completely off and then set back down again, and moorings that anchored the brick were dislodged, leaving all four brick walls unconnected to the house. Directly behind the Plummer's lot, at the Bristow residence (5 Hodgson Street), a board speared through the outside wall and into the partition beyond. A six-foot wall section flew eighty feet over a six-foot tall fence to lodge itself against the Hull residence at 1 Hodgson Street. Port Hope Fire Chief Jim Boughen reported that drywall cracked in homes up to a mile away.

The Bristow residence, 5 Hodgson Street.

OUR HOME CRUMPLED

Our home next door bounced, shook and shuddered, then crumpled like a pop can in a biker's grip. In three or four seconds, our delightful home dissolved into chaos. Yet, as though God held us in His hands, we were rocked up and down and from side to side in a kaleidoscope of confusion, but nothing touched us. Though our box spring snapped, we never even spilled our tea! (Can't waste a good cup of tea!)

In a rush of adrenaline, I lunged directly toward the explosion, bare-footed through the glass and ceramic strewn ensuite. The wash-room window framed a most eerie scene. The Plummer's 2500 square foot home had dissolved into a pile of sticks, hissing like a deflating plastic sea monster as it settled. I cried incredulously, "It's gone. The house next door is gone." But what of our neighbours, where were they? Nothing moving. No body parts. Nobody! Not even any dust lingering over the site. Nobody!

By peripheral vision and a slow deliberate turn, I began to drink in the devastation around me — walls gone, ceramic shattered, fixtures smashed.

Diane had disappeared from the bedroom. She had run to the back door — now wide open despite the lock. She called to our neighbour, Wes Harrison, "Is anyone there? Is anyone hurt?" Then, without waiting for an answer, she ran back upstairs.

The eerie scene Ray Cross first saw out of his washroom window seconds after the explosion.

Completely overwhelmed and disoriented, we were almost unaware of each other as we wandered aimlessly in what was left of our bedroom.

Then a call to reality —

"Is anyone there?"

"Yes. We're OK!"

"Get out of there! Now! I'm a firefighter. I know about these things! GET OUT OF THERE!"

It was Rob Pople, a neighbour and off-duty Markham firefighter, calling through our front door that now stood wide open with deadbolt fully extended.

Strange to say, neither Diane nor I had felt any change in temperature since the outside came in, but our neighbour's insistence spurred us to action. Since now all our windows were wide open to the world, I slipped a shirt and pants over my pyjamas. Diane couldn't reach her clothes. The wall had fallen on her dresser, throwing the hutch mirror on the floor and blocking access to the drawers. "I'm NOT going out without my clothes! I'm not going out without my CLOTHES!" she insisted. I put my back under the hanging wall and lifted while she rifled through drawers for something to wear. We chuckled about the lunacy of this even at the time.

When the explosion erupted the Crosses were enjoying tea on the bed in the foreground. The explosion blew in and out from the windows on each side of the bed, and across the end of the bed, through the washroom door to the right and behind the photographer.

BEFORE (August)

AFTER (November 10)

DAY OF CONTRASTS

November 10, 1993 was a day of strange contrasts. As Diane and I stepped through the gaping door of our shattered home, we entered a cluttered world of near stillness, no breeze, little movement — hushed as though holding its breath. Doors were opening throughout the subdivision as people spilled into the street. The din of voices increased gradually. A siren wailed in the distance.

People as bewildered as we milled about outside. Others plunged into the Plummer's lot in case a rescue was required. As more and more concerned and curious people arrived, pandemonium descended on the scene.

Practical considerations were my first concern. Realizing the need for personal transportation, the fact that service crews might block in my cars, and the need to make room for rescue vehicles to access the property, I backed one of my battered cars over the rubble in my driveway and parked it in a cul-de-sac down the hill. When I returned to Diane, the crowd had swelled and screeching fire trucks were arriving.

With the squeal of sirens and pulsating lights, firefighters and police swept in with practiced precision, to cool embers, clear clutter and control the growing crowd.

AND THE FIRES RAGED

The two fires as seen from the backyard of 5 Hodgson Street.

Hundreds of shocked residents clogged traffic throughout the area and clustered behind yellow ribbons on Ravine Drive.

By now fires had ignited in the rubble — on the west side of the Plummer's foundation, where the gas had entered their home, and at the north-east corner, nearest our home. The kitchen area fire, nearest our wall, appeared determined to spread. It spawned belching black smoke visible as far away as Cobourg. The blackest smoke and most vigorous flames belched from the Plummer's fridge, which would have been across the kitchen from the dishwasher. I said to Diane, "What we didn't lose to the explosion we may now lose to the fire." But with the help of a water cannon both fires were promptly extinguished.

*A water cannon dowses the flames at the gas point-of-entry
to 32 Ravine Drive*

Then firefighters boldly picked through the rubble to find the spot where gas entered the cratered foundation — ***not* a job I'd relish!**

While some firefighters wrestled the blazes, others sought to minimize dangers that might exacerbate the situation. Crowds were pushed behind plastic ribbons that cordoned off regions considered dangerous.

I intercepted one firefighter on his way to our home to check our gas installation. I assured him that, since our home was all electric, it constituted no risk. At the same time, I answered his questions concerning the place the gas installation entered the Plummer's foundation.

Flames dissolve into billows of steam under the relentless hoses of Port Hope firefighters.

Firefighters clear rubble to get at hidden embers.

A front end loader begins pushing debris back from the street.
Vivian MacDonald and neighbours in the foreground.

To this point, we'd been focused on the catastrophe next door and the possibility that someone was injured or killed. As evidence mounted that all were safe, we turned to scope damage to our residence....

OUR HOME TARGETED

The pattern of the explosion suggests that it targeted our home through the Plummer's bay window — directing two major thrusts, one at the garage and the other toward the north-west corner. So, it's not surprising that it looked as though someone had thrown a grenade against the west wall of our garage and a great beach ball at the laundry room.

B E F O R E

A F T E R

*The view from the roof of the incredible explosion-surviving shed built by
Dave Watts, the previous owner of 32 Ravine Drive.*

The garage west wall had disappeared. Any brick that remained
was pitted and hanging. The power stack attached to it hung like a
peeled banana. The power meter vaporized, leaving only the serial
number. (Electric clocks stopped at 9:32 a.m.)

The garage west wall of 30 Ravine Drive. A roof truss in the foreground. In the upper section you can see the suspended floor of Andrea's bedroom drooping into the garage. To the left, a sagging door frame.

Our power meter hangs low among the bricks, its neck broken, its face smashed. A piece of aluminum soffit lies folded in the foreground.

Two metres of 1" x 12" aspenite protrude from the corner of 30 Ravine Drive. Siding is severely perforated. The tubular steel television tower curves inward to follow the new contour of the wall.

A vertical view up the exterior laundry room wall of 30 Ravine Drive shows the concaved pattern of the bricks. When bricks are laid, mortar oozes into the holes in the bricks creating concrete dowels that lock the bricks together. Here some of the dowels have been snapped, knocking some bricks out of the wall, while others have spun on the hinges of surviving dowels.

Crinkled vinyl siding swings in the wind at the base of the television tower of 30 Ravine Drive. A brick tethered to and anchoring plastic wall sheathing appears to levitate, to the right.

One 2" x 12" beam had speared through the powder room window. The section of brick wall that struck the north-west side concaved the wall and pretzeled the television tower.

Shrapnel swiss-cheesed second floor vinyl siding. A board sliced through the upper corner like a knife through cake, and clothing sucked through the wall from the walk-in closet flapped in the breeze. (Workmen nailed through one of Diane's blouses when securing the building.) Corrugated eaves draped the edge of a garbage dump roof littered with torn shingles, shredded boards and gaping holes. Almost all windows in the house had been blown in, protecting them from breakage but destroying the jams. Pieces of the house and furnishings next door lay leaning against our walls and scattered over the lot.

The west side yard of 30 Ravine Drive.

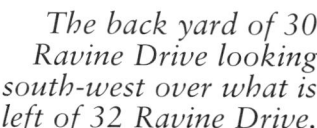

The back yard of 30 Ravine Drive looking south-west over what is left of 32 Ravine Drive.

EXPANSION AND CO-EXISTENCE

Both cars parked in our driveway were pummelled with projectiles, breaking windows and damaging almost every panel. In the midst of the rubble between houses — a book from the Plummer's library with the ironic title, *Expansion and Co-existence.*

WALLS SUCKED AND SUSPENDED

Inside, where Diane and I had been during the explosion, the east wall of the master bedroom had been sucked into the room. The west corner of the walk-in closet was gaping wide.

Because it no longer met the outside west wall, the floor was suspended by internal walls alone. The main washroom exterior wall had catapulted inward. A sheet of aspenite had knifed up the roof, slicing through and under the skylight.

The west wall of Andrea's bedroom had blown in, snapping the 2" x 4"'s on the bias. Her dresser mirror exploded into darts that pelted the desk on the other side of the room, and filled its sucked-open drawers with glass. Furnishings from both sides fell on the bed in the middle and the floor sagged into the garage.

Andrea's room. The wall bent and broken. Furnishings piled on the bed by the explosion.

Jeremy's room. Windows blown in and the snapped ceiling on the bed.

In Jeremy's room, the ceiling fell on the bed. Between those bedrooms the wall bowed several inches.

The 2" x 12" spear through the powder room window sliced off the top of the door and propelled it twelve feet down the hall.

CABINETS UNRAVELLED

Laundry room cabinets and appliances buckled and unravelled from the beach-ball blow.

The double-car garage was a pile of bricks of two distinct types, as many from one house as from the other. The steel door frisbeed to

The speared powder room door.

the inside wall. At the other end of the house, our piano bounced several inches across the carpet, walls cracked and ceilings sagged.

The debris strewn garage of 30 Ravine Drive, filled with boxes packed for our move.

Cabinets, wallboard and debris fill the laundry room.

AND THE PINK SNOW FELL

And the pink snow gently fell — fibreglass pink. Not one batt survived. All were blown to wisps and powder. And the powder went ballistic, then descended on a hushed east breeze in a fine rosy mist that wove a carpet to honour the occasion, broadloom laced with glass shards, bits of wood, protruding nails, personal papers and a grocery list. Roofs became snow cones; trees and bushes candy-floss. Workers raked it into drifts and vacuumed it up.

Pink fiberglass 'snow' blankets the ground. Dense smoke and steam obliterate all view of the remains of 32 Ravine Drive.

That day the *Port Hope Evening Guide* stated that a pile of rubble and a wisp of smoke was all that remained of the Plummer's home. The next day it reported that the blast destroyed two homes and seriously damaged about twenty others.

The Toronto Sun declared that the blast brought...

Total destruction

LEVELLED ... An explosion destroyed two homes and damaged about 20 others in Port Hope yesterday. Right: Scott Plummer and Vivian MacDonald, along with Vivian's son Marc, recover possessions from their razed home.

- Joe Warmington, Sun

By JOE WARMINGTON
Toronto Sun

PORT HOPE — The thunderous boom occurred as Vivian MacDonald was telling her students of the gas fumes that kept her awake most of the night.

"I made the bad joke that it was probably my house," she said yesterday about two hours after everything her family owns was blown into oblivion.

Her husband Scott Plummer and her sons Marc, 13, and Matthew, 2, had just left the Ravine Dr. home less than an hour before the blast.

Her home had been converted to gas the day before and MacDonald said the family had complained to the installer the previous evening.

With the exception of some personal pictures she found in a mound of debris, everything was lost.

But had the 9:30 a.m. explosion occurred an hour before everyone would have still been inside the house.

MacDonald, said it was by chance her husband wasn't home because the owner of Port Hope's IDA drug store is off on Wednesdays.

A shaken Marc feverishly searched for an Eric Lindros autographed rookie card, his baseball championship medal and a baseball signed by the 1993 Blue Jays. But he could only find his soaked Maple Leaf pyjamas.

'A miracle'

"It's a miracle that somebody wasn't hurt or killed," said Port Hope Fire Chief Jim Boughen, who says in 19 years with the volunteer force he has "never seen anything like this."

The blast destroyed two homes, seriously damaged about 20 others, left

PORT HOPE GAS BLAST SMASHES SUBDIVISION

the new subdivision looking like a war zone.

Pieces of one home flew several hundred metres in every direction and in some cases landed inside other homes.

Wood, glass and nails could be seen everywhere. Rooftops and lawns looked like they had been hit with a fresh snowfall of insulation.

But even with the devastation MacDonald, who is pregnant with her third child, still managed a sense of humor.

"You can tell my eighth-grade class that their history projects are gone so everybody gets an A," she joked as she sifted through the rubble of their former 3,000 square-foot-home.

Central Gas area general manager Paul Pastirik said it's too early to determine if natural gas was the cause. "I have no idea what happened," he said.

Port Hope police and fire officials, as well as everyone affected, insist such an explosion had to be from natural gas — especially since it was installed in the home less than 24 hours earlier.

"We could smell a sulphur smell about an hour after it was installed," said MacDonald. "But when my husband called about it, they said there was nothing wrong — it was just the newness of the equipment."

Enormous blast

Neighbor Wes Harrison, whose backyard abuts the MacDonald's, said the blast was so enormous that "I thought the house was coming down on me.

"I thought a bloody airplane had hit the house," said Harrison, who is relieved that he was in the basement. "It shook everything."

Inset: Scott Plummer, Vivian MacDonald and son Marc.

CHAPTER THREE

MEMORIES OF
NOVEMBER 10

Unforgettable memories sear the minds of many exposed to the devastation of that day. Though for us the explosion pulsated like a beating heart, those farther from the centre experienced only one shock wave. People miles away speak of the sensation of an earthquake or something bashing into the side of their building. Even Cobourg, twelve kilometres away, felt the blast and saw the plume of smoke. Homeowners throughout the area reported that their houses bounced, pictures and mirrors fell off walls, then they heard a crash of breaking glass, a thundering shower against walls and roofs and screams of terror.

As usual, Vivian MacDonald was on a hilltop less than a kilometre away beginning her school day at Dr. Hawkins Senior Public School. The moment life as she knew it dissolved, Ms. MacDonald was preparing her class for the eleventh hour in the eleventh day in the eleventh month, the day and time set aside to remember the heroes and horrors of war. To her class she was reading the famous Canadian Remembrance Day poem, "In Flanders Fields." Then, like an earthquake, the whole school shook. The floor shook. The windows shook. Everyone stopped. No one knew what it was, but Vivian suspected.... She blurted out what she considers a bad joke, "It was probably my house." Though afraid to look, she walked to the north end of the school and stared out the window. There before her unbelieving eyes were smoke and flames where a few moments before her gorgeous home had stood. Then she knew. It had to be. It was too much to be coincidence. Though told that this doesn't happen, she soon learned that it does — it did — to her.

"I WAS THERE!"

Elaine Large lunged through the front door of 10 Hodgson Street to see pieces of house raining from a billowing pink cloud. Realizing instinctively that its cause was gas, she bundled her family into the car and raced out of the area through a pink blizzard.

"I can't find them," said a rushing Robert Sculthorpe. Robert hadn't been home directly across the street from the explosion but his youngest son, Jeremy, and the baby-sitter were. "I'm told they're all right, but I can't find them."

While on location covering the story, a shaking Peggy Foster, staff reporter for the Port Hope Evening Guide, noticed, that day, that Gord Woods, who has a fair complexion, looked especially white, almost like parchment. She ventured, "This is quite the thing, eh

Gord?" With eyes wide, staring, he exclaimed, "I was there!"

That Wednesday morning, Gord's wife was scheduled for line dancing at Community Care. Normally another driver took her, but Gord chauffeured that day. On the way, he and Muriel stopped to pick up Dorothy Novinka. At approximately 9:30 a.m., November 10, Gord and Muriel pulled into the driveway of 34 Ravine Drive. The first thing they remember is seeing the front window of the Novinka's home blowing out toward them. (The front windows blew out; the back windows blew in.) Since Gord and Muriel were in downtown Port Hope during the major gas explosion 20 years before, they recognized the "whooshing" roar characteristic of gas explosions. They knew they had to get away.

As the shockwave engulfed her home, lifting its roof and dislodging all the brick from its moorings, Dorothy Novinka was approaching her front door. Though shaken by the blast, her first concern was for her dog; she ran to the laundry room to fetch him. Though situated at the end of the house furthest from the explosion, the door would not open. In a few seconds, after large chunks of debris had ceased falling, she burst through the front door.

Gord opened the driver's door, stepped out and called to her over his car. As she ran to the street, Gord backed out of the driveway. On the road, Muriel jumped out to grab Dorothy. She seemed in shock. Then Gord backed westward up Ravine Drive and parked, while Dorothy and Muriel ran away from the scene.

The Woods' car was covered with insulation. When Gord opened the door to yell to Dorothy, it invaded the interior as well. High speed particle damage pitted the paint and glass. The car was repainted and all glass, front, rear, and on the passenger side, had to be replaced. Yet no projectile touched a person, despite the glass that landed in Mrs. Novinka's slipper as she ran.

From his adjoining lot at 3 Hodgson Street, Wes Harrison stepped through the blown-in side door of his garage and looked straight up at "a great cloud of insulation as far up as [he] could see." Stephen Russell of 6 Hodgson Street sensed the "whooshing" surge, then darted for the door. While objects continued to hit the ground around him, Stephen ran down his driveway toward a billowing "funnel cloud of pink insulation." A mere fifteen seconds after the blast he was sifting rubble for bodies.

The view westward along Ravine Drive from the centre of the road in front of our home, 30 Ravine Drive.

While driving south on Highway #28, five kilometres north of town, John Floyd chanced to see a large puff of smoke rise from the Strathrose hill. But this smoke was different — pink in colour, with white in the centre and at the edges. It rose rapidly to what he estimates to be one hundred metres, mushrooming out at the top. Being familiar with Port Hope, he headed straight for the location, arriving before firefighters and police, and before the fires began. What he saw resembled a construction site, except in an unreal, helter-skelter state, with children's toys strewn about.

To his amazement, according to his report, "The house was not only missing, the foundation was completely bare."

The foundation of 32 Ravine Drive completely devoid of bricks.

At that very moment, Virginia Holmes, a resident at 6 Lyall Place, happened to be looking out her basement window. Since Lyall Place is much lower on the hill than the Plummer's, and since houses on both sides of Hodgson Street stood between her and 32 Ravine Drive, under normal circumstances, from that vantage point, it was impossible for her to see even the roof of the Plummer's house. Yet, after the explosion, she was able to describe the back of the Plummer's home and its kitchen windows. She said that the house lifted like a rocket from its pad, then shattered in all directions.

The Plummer's poured concrete foundation, broken and brickless.

Since it is evident that she saw the back of the house before it disintegrated, through triangulation, I estimate that the Plummer's home must have been propelled approximately five metres off the foundation before it burst. The description matches the evidence. I also observed that hardly one brick or board was left attached to the Plummer's foundation.

A TWO STAGE EXPLOSION

On-site evidence, as well as descriptions by John Floyd and Virginia Holmes, support a different scenario than that proposed by the Fire Marshal's investigation. The Plummers were apparently aware that the source of the fumes was in the furnace area of the basement, for they had kept the basement windows open all night. To reduce seepage to the rest of the house, where the family was sleeping, Vivian would have closed the door to the basement. In fact, the design of the Westchester model requires that the basement door be closed at all times when not in use so as not to impede normal traffic flow though the hall and up the stairs between the family room and kitchen. We know this because both the Plummer's and our home were the same model and floor plan. This means that when windows were closed that morning, the basement door would have likely been closed. During the hour the home was unoccupied, therefore, the richest mixture of gas would have accumulated in the basement of the home.

In my opinion, the explosion began here. If the explosion had begun in the first storey kitchen as the Fire Marshal proposed, the first stage of the blast would have pushed downwards on the first floor, and outward and upward everywhere else. The house would have exploded from the middle first, leaving the basement level bricks more intact. That is not what happened.

Eye witnesses saw the complete house rise into the air. This would require an immense force pushing upward on the basement ceiling — an explosion of sufficient power to lift the whole house off the foundation, bricks and all, and to blow apart the poured concrete foundation toward our home.

Then, in a fraction of a second, the flames would seep under the basement door and up the ducts into the rest of the house. A two stage explosion would be the result — one to launch 32 Ravine Drive off its foundation; the second to blow it to pieces.

Few of the Plummer's personal effects or clothes survived the explosion, perhaps because every cavity and the space between every fibre had tanked up on the gas. Stephen Russell, one of the neighbours who attacked the rubble looking for bodies before the fires started, said the blast "just consumed everything." The whole area resembled a war zone: houses and lots bombed, battered and broken. How quickly beauty turned to ashes!

As I stood behind the fireline, Scott Plummer approached the scene, walking as though the weight of a house were on his shoulders.

"Was there anyone in there, Scott?" I asked.

"I think so," he whispered.

"Oh, no!" I moaned.

My thoughts were of his wife and children; his of servicemen that were to visit that morning. If they had even been near the residence at the time of the blast they would have been cut to pieces. After viewing the damage, Scott left and returned shortly with his wife, Vivian, having picked her up from the school across the valley to the south. Since Vivian was severely shaken and four months pregnant, Scott took his wife first to be examined at the Port Hope General Hospital before returning with her to the devastating scene.

When things seemed under control, I left Diane for the home of Elgin and Gwen Ball, where I phoned my insurance agent and Mr.

Harrison, the lawyer for Mr. and Mrs. Klein, who had so appreciated the beauty of our home that they wanted to own it. After repairing a flat tire, I rejoined Diane, who had been mixing with neighbours in the crowd growing on the hill, swapping stories of what the explosion had done in each of their homes and where they had been and what they had experienced at the time of the explosion.

Who could doubt that miracles still happen? If building lots had not been so spacious, devastation would have been far more complete. Our home would have folded like a house of cards, crushing us in its grip. Ravine Drive was a favourite walking route for many, but no one was strolling by at the time. Though objects flew with lethal force, none found flesh.

In the midst of the melee, interviewers recorded responses on tape and video.

"It's a disaster but not a tragedy," said a shaken, but coherent Vivian MacDonald. She praised God that all were safe: the servicemen, the neighbours and all in her family. "We have everything to be thankful for. I'm so grateful that we're all alive. This makes us realize how lucky we are." From her own experience, she offered advice: "The firefighters told me that when I smelled gas I should have called the fire department. But we called the gas company instead because we didn't know. This is a chance to educate people to call the fire department if they smell gas."

Port Hope Fire Chief Jim Boughen, who in his 19 years with the volunteer fire department had "never seen anything like this," spoke of the miracle that not one was injured or killed.

Town Engineer John MacKay echoed Chief Boughen's remarks,

"I've never seen anything like it and don't wish to see anything like it ever again."

On video to Bruce Anderson of *CHEX-TV Peterborough,* I blurted, "The good Lord was looking after us. We went through the whole explosion without as much as a scratch. There isn't even any dust on us."

By the afternoon, the *Port Hope Evening Guide* reported that, between hugs from consoling

Ray And Diane Cross during CHEX-TV interview.

friends, all Vivian was able to salvage of her possessions was an address book and a cow-shaped cookie jar.

While emergency forces raced to the scene and wrestled with the blaze, Mayor Betty Collins, Town Clerk Michael Rostetter, Town Engineer John MacKay, Police Inspector Sam McReelis, Fire Chief Jim Boughen and a number of officials from the town building department gathered at the Emergency Measures Command Centre in the Port Hope Police Station. After a brief consultation, all proceeded to Strathrose Estates. In accordance with emergency procedures, Mayor

Betty Collins and Town Clerk Michael Rostetter arrived offering much appreciated assistance and accommodation to all affected. Crews were dispatched by the Town to clean up the neighbourhood and to board and secure nearby homes. Schools were contacted to forewarn students from venturing into the Strathrose area during the lunch hour. Efforts were made to track down and inform out-of-town and at-work owners of homes in the vicinity. Police were placed on alert to patrol the area against any breach of security or vandalism.

No emergency plan is flawless. There were some who complained about inefficiencies in the 911 system and the response of the Town and the Fire Department. None, however, can deny that the fire was extinguished quickly. No one was injured during or after the explosion and the clean up was prompt and adequate. In my opinion, this is an exceptional report on such a devastating and confusing moment in Port Hope's history.

Neighbourliness was enhanced as each reached to the other for support. Immediately after hearing the explosion, Rev. Lloyd MacArthur of Grace Missionary Church ascended the hill and went door to door offering assistance. Then, on their own initiative and at their own expense, Grace Missionary Church members hauled tables from their Church to the site and provided lunch for emergency crews and affected residents. BJ's Deli and Davis' ValuMart also sent refreshments. Susan Dewhurst, a downtown clothing store, donated clothing to the Plummers. By that afternoon, Realtor Nancy Fair, who had negotiated their move to Strathrose in September, found the Plummers a nearby furnished house to rent. Other friends and neighbours pitched in to encourage and help. A shower was even held to supply basic needs to the family.

We were in more shock than we realized — too overwhelmed to respond intelligently to any offer of comfort or assistance.

THE STRATHROSE REGATTA

During this period we were barraged by other people also seeking entry to our home for investigation, insurance and construction reasons. For the next week, every time we returned to our home, more people wanted to get inside. It was enough to blow our remaining circuits. We felt more and more devastated and even violated by the process. For weeks afterward, Ravine Drive was a regatta of sight seekers who cruised by slowly or wandered over private lands pursuing unique vantage points. Even a Brinks money truck adjusted its route to survey the damage through bullet-proof glass.

As on-site demands subsided the day of the explosion, concern for loved ones ignited, especially for our children. We had no way of knowing how their day had gone, nor had we considered it to this point. Now, however, we were desperate to catch Jeremy and Andrea before they heard the news through media, leaving them with the anguish of worrying about our safety. On the afternoon of November 10, therefore, I phoned Oshawa where our daughter Andrea had been boarding since September. (She was starting in a new high school there until we could complete the sale of our home in Port Hope and move.) At the time of the call, Andrea was in school, so I asked one of the fine ladies in the Oshawa church I pastored to contact her. "Tell her that her home has blown up but her Mom and Dad are fine."

The rest of the day spun around working with firefighters as they cleared our home of rubble and rammed windows back into their frames, clearing the freezer of as much food as we could find in the pitch black darkness of the basement and shipping food and plants to a friend for storage, assisting the Fire Inspector with his investigation, negotiating insurance provisions, providing garage storage for a car without windows, grieving with the Kleins for the loss of "our" home and enjoying the hospitality of Elgin and Gwen Ball, at 6 Mitchell Street.

The shock for some came at the end of a day's work. For example, Sue Reinstra, of 14 Lyall Place, had no idea what had happened until she returned from work that evening. Upon entering her home, she discovered her Siamese cat spinning in circles on the living room carpet. For months afterwards her pet remained strangely affected by the intense fear it had experienced while caged in vibrating rooms. Likewise, the dog of one of her neighbours on Ravine Drive met its owners by crawling toward the door with its muzzle in the carpet.

CHAPTER FOUR

STRUGGLES COPING WITH LOSS

"I ALMOST LOST MINE"

Andrea recorded her view of those events in her journal:

*November 10 was a day I'll **never** forget! It started like any other day. I had my spare first period so I slept in 'til a quarter to nine. I woke up and as usual was instantly reminded that I was not at home and not with my family. Don't get me wrong, the people I board with are great, but they're not my parents, and their house is not my home and I miss those things.*

I left their home at around 9:30 a.m. to catch the bus. As I walked to the bus stop, I sang my song from the movie, "Newsies." It starts out, "So 'ats what they call a family." Little did I know that at that moment I almost lost mine. At the same time that I was walking to the bus stop, singing about missing my family and my home, the house next door to mine in Port Hope was exploding.

I did nothing in vocal music that morning, just sat around and talked. Lunch was long — I stood by the piano and listened to Steve [Cochrane] play, but there was a deep pain inside me. I missed my parents and I desperately wanted to go home.

When I got to my third period class, I was told I had been called to the office. I was a little ticked off and very defensive.

When I walked in the door, Mrs. Cullen was there to talk to me. I said, "Hi!" very cheerily. I sat down and she told me that she had some bad news. I said, "Oh?" and wouldn't even think about what that might be. Then she said, "First of all, no one was hurt." My mind was blank. She told me that that morning, my next door neighbour's house blew up and there was a lot of damage to my house as well. All I could say was, "Oh."

I started asking her questions but she didn't know very much. I wasn't going to cry but it only took a few minutes for the full force of what she said to sink in. I began to cry and she gave me a hug. As the time went by, the tears came stronger and the pain dug deeper and I finally agreed for her to take me to my place. I cried some more, and tried to imagine what had happened.

The expression "blew up" is such an overrated expression. I recalled Mr. Court telling us in vocal music that morning that the computer in the music office "blew up." He said, "I walked into the room and the monitor had brown patches all over it and there was smoke in the air." "If that's the definition of 'blew up,' then it shouldn't be that bad," I told myself. Many pictures flashed through my mind: their [the Plummer's] house all burned, a big hole in the ground where their house used to be, but I never pictured anything wrong with my house and my pictures didn't even come close to what had really happened.

[While she was collecting her belongings at her locker, several friends passed by.]

Long hair comes in handy at times like these. Unfortunately, I began to cry again and long hair doesn't muffle sounds of sobs and I knew they all heard me. I shut my locker quickly and headed for the door, avoiding looking at any of them. Rob [Wildeboer] said, in the quietest and most serious and concerned voice I'd ever heard him use, "Bye Andrea."

Mrs. Cullen dropped me off at my place [in Oshawa]. The moment I walked in the door everything flooded down on me and I cried like I haven't cried in years. I sobbed and bawled and just laid on my bed. I must have cried for an hour and a half before I exhausted myself enough that I couldn't cry any more. I just lay on my bed in a daze. Finally I fell asleep.

The phone woke me around 4 o'clock. The sleep did me a lot of good; it rejuvenated me a little and gave me the strength to hold back my tears.

[Bill Wray, the Chairman of the Deacons' Board at Harmony Road Baptist Church, Oshawa, offered to drive Andrea to Port Hope.]

The drive down [to Port Hope] was excruciatingly long. When we finally got there, the neighbourhood was a circus. We had to park on the corner of Jocelyn Street and Ravine Drive. As I walked down the street, I couldn't believe all the people. Familiar and unfamiliar faces everywhere. It was really strange to see my quiet neighbourhood transformed into a tourist trap.

The police line was pulled across the street right at the Ross' yard [33 Ravine Drive] and there was a crowd of people standing at it. It was strange to step through the crowd and under the line, to be the centre of that kind of attention.

My heart was pounding but my chest felt like it had stopped. I was scared to round the last corner.

[Andrea has never been able to write more.]

WIDE-EYED ACROSS THE STREET

When we first caught sight of Andrea, it was dusk and she was standing wide-eyed in the crowd across the street, uncertain she had the right to cross the line to enter her own home. When we stepped out the door with possessions we were gathering for immediate needs, there she was, transfixed, helpless and hurting. We beckoned. She came. We melted in each other's arms. We had each other. For the moment all else paled.

Unbeknown to us, Andrea had carefully planned her bon voyage to 30 Ravine Drive. Her years there had been sweet. Like Snoopy, some of her fondest memories were of sitting on the roof enjoying the incredible view. She had planned to ascend to her thinking spot that weekend to say a fond farewell to her beloved home. But Wednesday wiped that possibility away. She would never go home again, period. Never again would she sleep in her room, in her home. One bang had shut the door with face-flattening finality.

The house she entered that November 10 was no longer her home, endearing because of its association with light and warmth and love. Now it was a cold, dark, windy place of disorder and desolation.

After a brief visit she returned to Oshawa, while we remained in Port Hope. How could she grasp the abrupt changes to her life? It was so unreal — so overwhelming. She describes that night as the only time she not only cried herself to sleep, but woke up crying as well.

A VINE CUT OFF

For our son, Jeremy, November 10 began as usual, attending classes at the University of Waterloo. When I called that afternoon to inform him of our circumstance, therefore, I was able only to leave a message on his answering machine. Andrea also called, but Jeremy knew nothing for fourteen hours. At 11:30 p.m., in blurring exhaustion, he fielded the life-shattering volley. What it all meant he could not fathom. Descriptions were inadequate. He was desperate to see it and us with his own eyes. On the way to class the next day, he picked up a newspaper. His whole world seemed reduced to front page headlines, pictures and words.

Friday afternoon, we collected Jeremy from Waterloo and Andrea from Oshawa. Andrea had experienced a brief time-warped visit to 30 Ravine Drive the Wednesday of the explosion, but to Jeremy it seemed so unreal as yet — he was desperate and impatient to ascertain for himself that his Mom and Dad were really all right and to see what was left of his home and his room. He needed to make it real. After a brief tour of the house, we settled as a family into the Comfort Inn for the weekend.

For Jeremy, so far from home base during the storm, the experience set him adrift. Like a vine, he had extended himself for the sake of his studies and now his root snapped off. He speaks of family and home as two great stabilizers of life. He had lost the second. Home is where the heart is — the explosion crushed not merely wood and brick, but his heart: "When you're afraid to go home, there's a loss of security. It's a factor not fully appreciated until its gone."

And mixed with this for both Jeremy and Andrea, was a sense of guilt that, though our family is so close, we weren't together at the moment of family crisis. Though none would choose to go through such an explosion, both would have sooner gone through it rather than hearing about it somewhere else from someone else. Both realized that they would not have been able to do anything if they had been there, but, as they described it, "It was our disaster too. We needed to be part of it — but we weren't, because we weren't there. We would rather have been there and been injured and even hospitalized than to be excluded from it. It was our disaster that we were forced to live with, but not through."

These thoughts seemed illogical to Jeremy and Andrea as well. They found them impossible to explain, especially concerning their motivation. Neither wanted the attention their being there may have brought them. Neither wanted to be there in order to be part of the action. Only when they shared with one another were their thoughts, feelings and responses affirmed as normal. Both had felt the same, independently. It was an awkward sense of separation. "We needed justification to feel the way we did, but we had none, because we did not go through it."

What aggravated their situation was that, from the parental perspective, separation and exclusion were both desirable. We openly thanked God that our children were not home. How could they explain to us their feelings? We made every effort to shield them from the stresses of the circumstance. We didn't want them hurt. But in doing so we excluded them, deepening their sense of isolation and intensifying the inexplicability of their mental state. They needed to be part of it; we wanted to protect them from it.

Geographic separation intensified this factor even further. Jeremy and Andrea were granted only brief glimpses of their precious home and then, continuing with their lives required Andrea to return to Oshawa and Jeremy to Waterloo.

For Andrea, it required coping with intense grief in a foreign environment: as a boarder in a new community, in a new school, with new friends who didn't really know or understand her.

For Jeremy, it meant re-immersion into his gruelling honours mathematics program at the University of Waterloo. The struggle was how to re-apply himself. It took everything he had to cope with that pressure even when life was on an even keel. This tidal wave overwhelmed him. The full concentration required was impossible. He was always concerned and drained, struggling with the unreal nature of his circumstance and his inability to do anything to help. When insurance provision began to fall apart within a week after the explosion, the stress and distance drove him to distraction.

Jeremy failed two courses. We appealed to the University of Waterloo for consideration due to stress and trauma. We did not ask that the two credits be granted, only that the failures not be counted against him lest they compromise his ability to remain in the honours program. The University absolutely refused. Though such allowance had been granted even to students who had lost girl friends, the loss of his home and the near death of his parents three weeks prior to exams were deemed unworthy of any consideration whatsoever. For months afterwards, Jeremy and I would walk into the wee hours of the morning talking through this and other disappointments and struggles.

During the recovery period Jeremy received comfort and encouragement from close Christian friends and fellow students. Andrea had no such luxury. While Jeremy had had more than a year to develop friendships in Waterloo, Andrea had been in Oshawa for merely two months. She found that everyone in the school already had their friends. She was a grade twelve student in the midst of hundreds of other students, none of whom really knew her or understood her. She discovered that everyone likes a happy person, but has little time for an acquaintance who is hurting:

People quickly forget the news. They expect victims to do the same. They even have expectations as to how we should think and act in such circumstances. We can't react our own way — whatever that might be for each individual. To fail to fit their mould is to whine. But, for me, my life fell apart November 10, and time stood still. The world went on without me. Yet it expected me to keep up. "Oh! I'm sorry! That's life. Carry on." What was I to do with all this baggage while I tried to keep up? I tried to share it with others so they could help me but they didn't care enough to be patient enough to listen enough until I healed. I was allowed only a certain amount of time to mourn — a time they set for me. In fact, most didn't know how to respond. Pictures of the event were so bizarre that some treated them with amusement.

CHAPTER FIVE

EXTENDED CONSEQUENCES

FITFUL SLEEP

We arranged accommodation at the local Comfort Inn but neither Diane nor I slept well that first night. Noises startled. An overactive mind woke me at 5:00 a.m. Since Comfort Inn was now our home, I put on my house coat and made my way to the motel lobby for coffee, to write in my journal and to jot down the many new responsibilities required by the events of the previous day. We'd need to cancel telephone, power and water. We would need to contact the tax department for a new tax status. We would need to contact other relatives and friends to apprise them of our situation. The Building Inspector desired a tour. The car insurance company had to be contacted to begin arrangements for replacement or repair....

The rest of the week, nights were short — no more than five fitful hours of sleep. We were easily disturbed. Each morning began with a headache. Every waking moment was consumed with urgent details from dawn to dark: dealing with telephone, utilities, taxes, car repairs, engineers, investigators, the real estate lawyer, the purchasers, house and car insurance adjusters, our doctor, the motel, friends, relatives and parishioners. Within a week after the explosion, a beloved parishioner died. I performed the funeral.

Each night we slept a little better, but not long. We felt constantly drained and experienced headaches often.

That Sunday I preached from one of my favourite Bible verses, Luke 1:79: [Jesus came] *To give light to them that sit in darkness and in the shadow of death, to guide our feet into the way of peace.*

Inner peace is granted us when we put our faith and trust in Jesus. Walking in that peace is not an absence from perplexity, but is rather a product of continuing to love the Lord and to do God's will despite the confusion that sometimes surrounds us. It is a matter of inner trust, that God will work all things together for our good because He loves us and because we remain committed to Him.

On Monday, Building Inspector Ken Andrus stated that our home needed support walls to protect it from collapsing. Until they were installed he would "card" the house: "Unsafe, No Trespassing." Not even we would be permitted in our home until the card was removed. Not only had our house been damaged, now our home and possessions were out of reach.

When we finally gained access, it was nothing to celebrate. It meant days of sorting through piles of bricks, clothes-strewn closets and damaged possessions in a dark, damp, cold building littered with glass, drywall and insulation. There was so much to do, yet the more we worked, the worse things looked. It only added to our disorientation and discouragement.

A NERVOUS COMMUNITY

The shock of November 10 made the whole community nervous. The week following there were two anonymous calls reporting the smell of gas on the hill and one evacuation of fifty homes, but leaks were not found. In another section of town, the smell of spilled gasoline prompted a false alarm.

Ontario Fire Marshal Inspector, Gene Szabo, firefighters and Centra Gas officials sifted through the mounds of rubble at 32 Ravine Drive for two days to determine the cause. The investigation, under authority of the Fire Marshal's Office and the fuel branch of the Ontario Ministry of Consumer and Commercial Relations, determined that the weakness was in piping to a gas furnace and water heater installed by Watson's Heating. The company's licence was revoked and charges laid.

INSURANCE RESPONDS

Householder reports of insurance company performance in meeting needs of policy holders vary widely. Some were prompt, efficient and accommodating. Robert and Heather Sculthorpe, whose home directly across the street caught the Plummer's front door between its second storey windows, reported that the day of the explosion their insurance company hired someone to inspect the roof and clean up glass. Garry Hull, of 3 Hodgson Street, said his company did even more than he expected or requested. The Plummers, who, despite their anguish, retained their sense of humour, reported a week after the explosion that, "Everything was still up in the air." But plans were already under way for clean up. An article in the *Port Hope Evening Guide* recorded the progress.

Bigger and better — Dennis Macklin is one of the workers who is helping to reconstruct the Plummer-McDonald house on Ravine Drive blown up by a gas explosion in November.
Photo by Ted Amsden

Work continues to repair gas-explosion damage

By Peggy Foster

Some of those who suffered property damage in the Nov. 10 gas explosion on Ravine Drive are recovering more quickly than others.

The explosion demolished a house at 32 Ravine Dr. owned by Scott Plummer and Vivian McDonald. A new house being built on the site has walls and a roof and is expected to be ready for occupancy by early March.

"I have to give (builder) Don Pocock credit," Ms. McDonald said last week. "They got started in the good weather in December and worked through Christmas and on weekends."

While the question on everyone's lips is whether the couple will have natural-gas heat in their new home, neither Ms. McDonald nor Mr. Plummer would comment publicly.

The family is renting a house on Ontario Street while work on their new home continues.

Meanwhile the house next door at 30 Ravine Dr., owned by Ray and Diane Cross, sits empty, with plastic covering its western exterior. Part of the west wall was knocked in by the force of the explosion from the Plummer-McDonald house.

The Crosses moved to Oshawa after the explosion but still own the Ravine Drive home.

Mr. Cross said last week that his insurance company is still trying to assess what to do with the house.

"I just don't know what will happen," he said.

The people of Harmony Road Baptist Church in Oshawa, where he is the pastor, have been very supportive, he said.

"The people here have stood with us through this tough time and that's just what we needed."

He described what he saw on a recent visit to the Ravine Drive home as a sad situation. There were still garage doors missing on homes and the street appeared to be in disarray, he said.

Edward and Dorothy Novinka, who own the home immediately west of the explosion site, at 34 Ravine Dr., say they expect to move back in by the end of February.

While the brunt of the blast was directed to the east, the Novinkas' home also received major damage. All of the bricks on the exterior had to be removed and replaced because they had shifted, Mrs. Novinka said.

Drywall inside the home also shifted and had to be replaced, she said.

The Novinkas have been renting a home elsewhere in Port Hope for the last month.

"We're crossing the bridges as we come to them," Mrs. Novinka said.

Some insurance adjusters spoke of people attempting to make unjustifiable claims, but the ones I talked to in the immediate area exhibited no such motivation — they just wanted to get everything back to where it was so they could get on with their lives. The twenty-two households I surveyed were insured by eleven insurance companies. Seventeen of these were pleased with the service and settlements they received. Their assessments of care (not including mine) covered the whole gamut of opinion, from "excellent," to "pleased," to "good," to "OK," to "bad," to "a nightmare." Variables included promptness or delay, the deductible (some insurance companies waived it due to the utter innocence of insureds), respect or disrespect from insurance employees, stinginess or generosity and whether rates were affected. It was strange to discover that the size of claims was not the deciding factor in raised rates. Some did not raise rates despite a large claim, yet one company raised rates because of a three hundred dollar claim. Some companies volunteered to return the extra premium payments and the deductible if claim costs were retrieved through legal proceedings against those responsible. Due to dissatisfaction with the treatment they received, five out of the twenty-two households switched insurance companies. Three of the five who switched were insured with the same company that held our home policy.

INSURANCE BREAKDOWN

Our cars and home were insured by different insurance companies.

Though our car insurance company attempted to settle the car damage and replacement claims frugally, it remained negotiable. Within a short period of time, we reached an equitable settlement:

one car was replaced, the other repaired.

Concerning our home, we found little comfort in being insured.

After paying home insurance premiums for twenty-three claim-free years, our family was now in desperate need of the protection and provision for which we had paid.

Help arrived promptly.

How comforting to have our insurance agent on location almost immediately, assuring us that our "guaranteed replacement value" policy meant we'd be well cared for! A staff adjuster from our insurance company also arrived from Toronto promptly, let herself into our home while we were away, took pictures and then met with us at our insurance agent's office. There the adjuster summarized our insurance coverage. The insurance company would cover accommodation, costs of food above our normal expenses, moving costs, home repair or replacement costs, and replacement costs or depreciated value for possessions. She seemed genuinely concerned, offered us a $3000 advance for immediate expenses and authorized overnight accommodation.

The date for completion of our house sale was closing in fast. The contract permitted the purchasers to withdraw if the house was not in the same condition at time of closure as it had been at time of viewing. Boy! What an understatement! But they liked the house and the location. They tried to hold on, but to no avail. The insurance company was unable to work fast enough to clarify the Klein's and our legal position concerning the policy provisions. So, reluctantly the Kleins withdrew their offer to purchase. We were once again trapped by a house that would not let us go.

Months of turbulence followed as we sought to re-establish our household in rented accommodations, to repair one car and replace the other, to itemize loss, to protect, repair and replace possessions, to work with insurance adjusters, contractors and engineers in establishing building loss and reconstruction figures. What began as a thunder bolt, continued rumbling through each encumbered day and unsettled night. It was like wading a swollen stream with the current pounding against us every step of our rock-strewn way.

NO MOVING EXPENSES

A week after the explosion we were granted access to our home by the Building Inspector. I phoned the insurance adjuster to share how we were doing and to arrange our move. I confessed disorientation because we felt violated, vulnerable and exhausted. I suppose I expected sympathy and consideration — none was extended. Now she was all business. I asked if the insurance company would pay moving expenses, as the policy stated. She said, "No, because you were going to move anyway." While that was true, I pointed out that this was not the move we had planned. Our house now had no power, no heat, no light. Our possessions were damaged and in disarray. Food that Diane was unable to find in the dark was rotting in our freezer. Movers were now inadequate; we needed disaster relief. Had we known what every adjuster knows, (that intent prior to a loss can never legally be used to evade responsibility to honour any aspect of a policy's coverage) we would have argued the absolute legal necessity that our moving expenses be paid. But we did not know that. All we knew was that our insurance company was not providing the protection our policy promised.

To add insult to injury, she followed up with several comments that suggested our honesty would be suspect throughout our dealings.

NO WILL TO FIGHT

Our life had just shattered around us. We had been blasted into a bewildering world of insurance regulations and rights. And now we were not receiving the provisions our policy promised. We were in no state to defend ourselves and we knew it. We saw no option but to hire a public adjuster. Months later a claims representative for the insurance company challenged the wisdom of my choice of representation, stating that I would have been treated better by the company if I had appealed to the executive level rather than going beyond the company for help. In normal circumstances, I might have agreed with him, but he represented that level, and despite our attempts to work with him to keep claim costs down, in our perception, he had worked only to reduce those costs even further, at our expense. From that level, to this point, I had endured arduous negotiations and received a written veiled threat that the company would not pay the claim at all (a letter called standard procedure for that company by the claims representative author), and our requests for advances or reimbursements were resisted strenuously or refused. He even stated that my case had been taken to the highest levels of the company and that they had approved of everything their adjusters and claims representatives had done to us. No, we needed a public adjuster to represent us and our interests against a company we had already paid for protection. (The insurance company paid our moving expenses without a peep as soon as the public adjuster became involved.)

THE LAST SCAR ON THE HILL

In many ways, the psychological warfare of those extended insurance negotiations was worse than the explosion itself. (I learned enough to write a book about insurance claims.) Nine months after the explosion, all other homes were repaired and 32 Ravine Drive rebuilt. Of the Strathrose explosion, our home remained the last surviving scar.

A view of 30 Ravine Drive though the Plummer's new bay window, March 1994.

The last scar on the hill — 32 and 30 Ravine Drive, April 1994. Even the lot of 30 Ravine Drive remains littered with bricks, glass, soggy dry wall and boards with protruding nails.

NO MEDIA COVERAGE

During those long months, the local paper, a major Toronto newspaper and a Toronto television station contacted us for our story. Not wanting to antagonize our insurance company, we did not pursue the coverage they offered. It was not our intent to stir up trouble; all we wanted was provision that would extricate us from the financial quagmire that had landed on our doorstep. But the insurance company showed no appreciation for our reserve, nor did they recognize its benefit to them until on April 7, 1994, we placed a sign in the window of our damaged home stating, in all capitals, "INSURED BY STATE FARM." It was my opinion that it was up to them whether this would prove to be good advertising or bad. The sign was posted to protest the posturing of an insurance company whose offers for settlement would, in our opinion, leave us with a loss of thousands of dollars. But it did something more. When a reporter arrived at our insurance agent's office asking the company's side of the story, an insurance executive phoned her in an attempt to polish its tarnished image, but the company's attitude toward our needs did not change.

What made our dealing with the insurance company doubly difficult was the intentional nature of the interaction. Whatever the factors that contributed to the disintegration of 32 Ravine Drive and its effect on our lives, there is no evidence that that event was planned, but everything our insurance company did was carefully conceived and implemented. Though they would rationalize it as responsible claim management, from our perspective, their tight restriction in releasing funds was malicious. Despite the fact we had all committed ourselves to abide by the decision of the Umpire that both the insurance company and we enlisted to mediate our differences, when he brought down his Appraisal Award decision, the insurance company defied him. We had to enlist the services of an insurance lawyer to enforce payment. That lawyer expressed utter dismay that our insurance company would be so difficult despite the almost definite prospect of their retrieving between 90 to 100 per cent of the loss through legal action they already had in place. He speculated that perhaps this manner of approaching major claims may be so habitual that this company finds it almost impossible to conceive of behaving otherwise.

Though not necessarily involving their insurance companies, many on the hill experienced similar struggles. Their lives, like ours, were disturbed and dislodged. Treasured possessions were damaged or lost. Unanticipated expenses intruded. Because the trouble arrived through no fault of their own, injustice gnawed at their soul. Both Joseph La Croix of 7 Hodgson Street and Elaine Large of 10 Hodgson Street expressed such disappointment and insecurity that for a time after the event they felt compelled to move. Had they succumbed to that obsession they might have compounded their problems by bailing out at great personal loss. Only with time did the urge subside.

CHAPTER SIX

INNER TURMOIL

A PROVEN TRACK RECORD OF STRESS MANAGEMENT

Life had been difficult enough for our family prior to the explosion. From the beginning, we had opted for challenge rather than comfort. During my first pastorate in Peterborough, I burned the midnight oil earning a second degree. In seven years, I led that church through growth that doubled its numbers. Prior to coming to Port Hope, my family and I had birthed a new congregation in Trenton. Despite challenges that pushed our every faculty to the limit, we persevered for twelve years, until Orchard View Baptist Church, Trenton, had grown from three families meeting in rented facilities to more than a hundred people meeting in their own building on 3 3/4 acres of land. The rigors of that ministry had weakened me physically and I had surgery a few months before beginning in Port Hope. Our brief ministry in The First Baptist Church of Port Hope involved leading them in renovating their ageing facilities in preparation for growth. That ministry ended abruptly leaving me out of work, on unemployment insurance for ten months. We were people with a proven track record of stress management and creativity despite duress, but nothing could prepare us for the complications that had landed on our doorstep.

As a Christian pastor, I have often been disappointed when people failed to value my counsel. Yet, when Port Hope Mayor Betty Collins gave advice to explosion victims, I felt her aim missed me, until its truth swept me away. On page two of the *Port Hope Evening Guide* of November 12, Mayor Collins advised, "They [the victims] should be aware that maybe in a few days or weeks a letdown or some sort of post traumatic disorder may set in. If they find themselves wondering what happened to them and why, they should not hesitate to seek professional help."

"That's not me. I've got myself and my life together. I've got the Lord. This is just an inconvenience related to external possessions."

BEGINNING TO CRACK

But aftershocks of the explosion shot fissures through our souls as complications *without* produced confusion *within*. The trauma of the blast, the raging torrent of life-altering decisions, the ego-shattering humiliation of being considered a credit risk for the first time in our lives because our resources were locked into a dilapidated shell, the dike-straining challenge of protecting our children from the full disintegrative force of our circumstance, and grief we felt for what we perceived as desertion by our insurance company, began tearing apart the seams of our psyches. We felt as though we were groping through an endless fog, trying to part the mists with our hands.

INVISIBLE DAMAGE

If our personal injury had been physical, both we and others would have seen the damage and understood the ailment and the treatment. But what happens when the wound is psychological and/or spiritual? Such injuries are invisible to the eye unless they produce unusual or antisocial behaviour. Even when this happens, understanding is not automatic. Not only are others prone to criticize and judge, but we may castigate our own inability to "snap out of it." Though invisible, psychological and spiritual injury is just as real and in need of healing, just as painful and in need of gentle and understanding therapy.

In the midst of troubles, there are always a few who, failing to appreciate the intensity of a trial, dump on others their simplistic assessments and advice. One such observed, "You're not practicing what you preach. You are supposed to trust God." Such people view theology statically, rather than recognizing that one's beliefs are tested in the crucible of life. They fail to recognize that relationships grow through shared experiences, even our relationship with God. I responded, "I trust God. The problem is I have to make the decisions." (In my shell-shocked condition that was incredibly exhausting because my own judgement and inner assurance were impaired.) Sometimes, therefore, when one's theology meets life's realities, it is not pretty, but neither is a cake until it's done. Yet we know enough not to criticize the messiness of a baker before the cake rises. Besides, I believe realism is what is needed, rather than a candy-coated Christianity that promotes evasion and denial.

Our family has a new understanding and empathy for those who go through tragedy. Our ordeal was more inconvenience than anything. We did not lose life or limb. We did not lose our health. We did not lose our marriage or family. We lost time to trouble. We lost our home and money. Nothing we lost was permanent — it could all be replaced. Yet it was inconvenience of such intensity that it consumed our lives for more than a year. It produced depressive psychological states. How then, I ask, do those who face true tragedy cope, especially in the presence of people who expect and even demand that they snap out of it. Through the heat of trial, we are convinced that never could we or should we deal with tragedy-induced anguish with anything but the greatest empathy and support.

HEART-WRENCHING GRIEF

Our whole family went through profound grief for the loss of a good friend — our home. It would not have been so difficult if we had left her with dignity, but we'd left her abruptly and in distress. Then she hung on the hill for months, injured, but insurance company complications rendered us unable to put her out of her misery or to extend a touch of healing. It was as though our heart had ceased beating when our clocks stopped at 9:32 a.m. Wednesday, November 10. There would be no real rest until we could sign the waiver for surgery or the death certificate, close the door and walk away for good.

If the normal pressures of life ceased for a while during and after tragedy, it would be easier to cope, but the normal and abnormal intermingle and amplify each other. We sometimes describe it as tragedies coming in threes. It is a knock-out punch to which many succumb. But we plodded on, step by arduous step, against the gale of complications that rolled over us in gravel-grinding breakers. Since our struggles demanded so much of our attention we had little time or energy for our inner turbulence. It was as though each step forward on the outside taunted the tornado within.

Much of what follows, Diane also experienced in greater or lesser degrees. Her mind, as mine, became preoccupied with the problems. She described it in terms of a video back-drop that ran continually through the subconscious and periodically invaded the conscious. Awakening each morning involved pushing past these mists of memory to cope with what each new day brought. For her, this involved loss of work and income due to our move and the fact that schools aren't inclined to hire supply teachers with no fixed address. Also, due to her mental distraction and the specific circumstances of a moment in time, our car, which had already been written off due to the explosion, was hit again while she was driving, doubly disposing of its exterior. It was another shock to shake her and us.

MONEY TROUBLES

Though we had always managed our finances responsibly and carefully, when we became vagabonds, we lost control. Expenses mounted and uncertainty about future necessities loomed like an ominous thunderhead. Because the insurance company manoeuvred to minimize its losses and to keep us off balance, we liquidated investments to meet expected and unexpected demands. When all of our funds were used up, we borrowed from relatives, from our children's education savings and from lending institutions. We ended up owing more money than ever before in our lives.

Though we had taught others how to budget, through no fault of our own, our finances were now completely out of control. These were changes so completely out of character with what our life had been to this point that our psyches began drifting, identity became blurred, fogging our minds beyond our ability to cope with required decisions. Discretion evaporated. Decisions blew up in our faces. Like the natural gas that changed our lives, we began to lose ourselves in our swirling surroundings.

CONFUSION REIGNS

What happens to organized minds when forced to live in a disorderly environment? It's a struggle faced by all displaced by disaster, deprivation or war. Like walking on marbles, life goes into flux. Where and how we live no longer expresses who we are. How and where we live is no longer a matter of choice but of imposed necessity. (In two months we lived in two towns, three motels and one house.) Extended separation from familiar walls and possessions is like being set adrift. We lose material moorings. Possessions lose permanence and become liabilities because there is no place to put them and no opportunity to use them. When we do need them, we are frustrated because they aren't where they used to be. We grasp for restoration but are destabilized because the familiar is difficult to retrieve. We oscillate between realizing the unimportance of possessions and intensifying our quest for the things we have lost.

SPACED OUT

For my part, the dematerializing of familiar matter before my eyes influenced my view of matter itself. It seemed a lesson in atomic realities. Though it looks solid, I had been taught that matter is really mostly empty space. For periods of time following the explosion, it seemed the atomic level took precedence. When I looked at things, I saw more space than substance. Cohesion seemed an illusion — the world, dizzying unreality.

NO ESCAPE

Most would book a holiday in Mexico for delight. We did so in desperation, leaving mid-January 1994, two months after the explosion. But the problems we sought to escape were as much in our minds as in our surroundings, and our heads took the trip with us. Trial had left us out of phase with ourselves. Though enjoying the warmth of the sun, the refreshment of a different culture and the unguarded friendliness of the people, for two weeks we walked like zombies through the streets of Puerto Vallarta.

When the two weeks expired, I came unglued. As Diane and I stood on the tarmac waiting to board our return flight, I began sobbing uncontrollably. We had spent two weeks with no concern but where to walk, where to eat, what to buy and how much sun to accept. Now we were returning to the insanity and anguish from which we had escaped.

On the plane, the turbid waves from which I had run washed over me. Though I had a window seat there was nothing to distract me from my grief. After the plane left Mexican air-space, the clear sky below became cloudy, so the ground and all of interest below disappeared. To make it worse, we had been scheduled to leave Mexico at 1:00 p.m., but a snow and ice storm in Toronto and a strong head wind had delayed our plane. While we appreciated extra time in Mexico, it meant our flight was through the night.

As we reached maximum altitude, we picked up the jet stream that had delayed the Toronto to Mexico flight, this time as a tail wind of more than 120 km per hour. As we rocketed through the heavens, it seemed we were charging down a dark tunnel to hell.

Hours of embarrassing emotion and tears vented the incapacitating stress within. As we drew closer to Toronto, my anguish subsided. I felt I would be able to cope with the challenges before us. Perhaps, I vainly hoped, the worst was over, but even if not, pain may be inevitable, suffering is a choice. However mixed up our circumstances in the past, our future course was clear — we must persevere to the end.

CHAPTER SEVEN

OPPORTUNITY IN TRAGEDY

In Chinese pictograph writing, the symbol for "crisis" combines characters meaning "danger" and "opportunity." If we have to experience crisis, we must determine not to miss the opportunities for personal growth and ministry it offers. Like a kite rising against the wind, to benefit by crisis we must allow it to work creatively, even if painfully, always vigilant for opportunities for progress through it. It is my hope that what we experienced and learned will assist others to traverse trials creatively.

NO HIDING

While in the middle of the trial, it would have been difficult to assess how well we were handling our ordeal, but having walked through tragedy and grief with many others through the years, I knew the answer was not in hiding from our feelings or keeping a stiff upper lip as though our struggles did not exist. This may impress some, but the personal price is too high. While feigning outward wholeness may feed our ego, in the midst of tragedy, it fragments us inwardly. Beneath a fabricated veneer of composure, our inside decomposes, then later bleeds forth in protracted grief, which is far more difficult to deal with than merely being honest with ourselves and others as we go through trial. So we focused on being real rather than socially acceptable or right by others' criteria. We have conscientiously tried not to drive repercussions deeper within by feigning composure.

We have been working it out and talking it out. It's been like peeling the onion of our inner life — rings within rings of emotional, psychological and spiritual anguish that must be vented through tears and talking, through relevant reading and prayer, through friendship and spiritual fellowship. It's been an untidy process, but necessary if all our pieces are to reconfigure in accordance with the demands of our new situation.

GRIEF MUST BE VENTED

We have been learning from experience that all forms of major loss create grief that will not be denied. We might try to hide from it or to put it behind us, but sooner or later we have to face it. Grief is like the gas that began this fiasco. Vented gradually, it does no damage, but when denied expression, it creeps into cavity after cavity of our soul until other shocks or loss spark release through mental instability, physical ailment or social alienation.

TALK, BUT TO WHOM?

So loss, and the grief it causes, may be either integrative or dis-integrative, depending on how we process it, and processing it constructively usually requires the help of others. Grief therapists teach the necessity of venting our anguish in the presence of supportive and sympathetic listeners. If we are not given the opportunity to do so, or if we fail or refuse to do so, pent up stress will not only rob us of resilience, but will contribute to the development of degenerative diseases.

Everyone in our family realized the need to talk out our experience, but struggled with inner ambivalence toward doing so. At one and the same time, we felt compulsion to discuss it, yet recoiled at the pain such sharing stirred up within. We seemed unable to forget it, unable to evade it, yet unable to face it either.

This was especially so between family members. As parents, we sought to shield our children from the full stress of our circumstances, yet in doing so we shut them out of the intimate sharing they craved. So, while we all went through different shades of the same shadow, we failed to blend them to our mutual comfort. What a loss! When we should have been the greatest comfort to one another (who would understand more fully?), we were isolated islands, harbouring hurts too complex for most to comprehend. It was not until 1 1/2 years after the blast that I sat down with Jeremy and Andrea in an attempt to understand how they were coping. Their response was like a crack in a dike — first a little, then more, then a gushing torrent of pent up anguish and astonishingly clear insight into the grieving process.

My problem, as theirs, was who could I talk to? Who would not only listen, but keep on listening as I shared the same things over and over? And who would understand? How could anyone who has not gone through what I have experienced really understand? I didn't want to have to explain or defend myself; I just wanted to talk with someone who was understanding! But in my circumstance, my occupation got in the way. I am a clergyman. I'm the one others come to with their problems. I'm the one that is so close to God that some forget that I'm not God, and have no desire to be equated with Him. I'm the one who is supposed to be able to face even overwhelming circumstances in the power of God alone, without human help or mediation. It's an illusion I cannot and will not live in, but how do I share my inner struggles without compromising my spiritual leadership? How do I survive in this tradition-imposed isolation? It's a problem intensified for me, but no less real for all who suffer tragedy and loss. A friend who lost a dear wife and child in an auto accident said, "It feels like being encased in a bottle, hopelessly yelling as loud as you can — no one really hears your exploding heart."

What is needed is formal fellowship groups or informal groupings of people who have experienced the same or a similar event. These should meet regularly, preferably under the constructive and supportive oversight of clergy or a grief counsellor. Because of their common experience and needs, participants will have vested interest in the process; they are there for themselves as well as for others. For the group to work, these people must commit themselves to each other, never sharing with anyone outside the group anything they should keep in confidence. Such people are most inclined to encourage virtually unlimited sharing between grievers of all aspects and issues of consequence to them. Such people will love each other out of their anguish. By doing this, pressure is released and personal damage reduced. Diagnostically, when the telling of your story becomes boring to you it means that it has lost its emotional baggage — you have healed. And as people heal, they are free to drift away into the mainstream again. When needs dissolve, so does the group.

JOURNALING

Even with good support from significant responsive people, there are aspects of anguish that may be too private to share, or that rise when no one is there. These also need to be released lest their acid consume our soul. For these, journaling may prove invaluable, since it offers the opportunity to drain off damaging attitudes and emotions in a non-judgmental environment. When nightmarish worries overwhelm, dump them without reserve on the privacy of the written page. When perplexity invades, writing it often clarifies issues and actions necessary to solving it. If you are not inclined to write, it matters not. You write for yourself, none other. You write to release, nothing more. You write and write until the story is empty of emotion.

When I speak of journaling, I do not refer to books or bindings. Pages in a loose leaf binder will do. In fact, the less ostentatious the format, the more uninhibited your writing will probably be. Don't write to be read — write to release. Don't worry about form, appearance or grammar, just let it flow out freely on the page. The only consequence you pursue is inner stability, not fame or favour. Let it out in any words that come — then save, or use or discard them. It doesn't matter as long as you heal.

REKINDLED MEMORIES

Since that fateful day, November 10, 1993, explosions have shattered the lives of Ontarians in Pickering, Scarborough, Oshawa and Hamilton, not to mention the horrific destruction in Oklahoma City. Each of these events, or even the sound of a siren, is like a spark in the tinder of our memory. To the degree they re-ignite our original anguish, they indicate lack of healing. More sharing and caring are required.

Also, it is well established that our systems have built in chronometers. On the anniversary of disaster, therefore, we may sink into emotional states similar to those experienced the year before. The first thing to recognize is that this is normal. It's called annual disease. Since anxiety intensifies the problem, don't worry about it. The best therapy is to be kind to yourself and accept your state without complaining. Each year try to take the edge off your feelings to soften their hurtfulness. By being gracious and considerate to yourself, over a period of years you will raise the emotional altitude of these valleys.

RELATIONSHIPS PRIMARY

Pressure comes between only if we allow it. From any other direction, pressure pushes us together. So, recognizing that the essence of life is not bound up in the things we possess, major on relationships. Keep the pressure behind, with love, appreciation and encouragement between. Cling to relationships crucial to quality living — to family, to friends, to the Lord. In these is security — especially in the Lord, since even death cannot rob us of our relationship with Him.

WHAT YOU THINK, YOU ARE

Difficulties of life do not leave us unchanged; we emerge either bitter or better. (The difference between the two is "I".) The notions we form of situations may damage us more than the circumstances themselves. Even when we are at the bottom, there are other ways to go than up. We may go sideways within our trial, keeping ourselves in the problem rather than rising out of it. While solving complications without, we may actually nourish and perpetuate their destructive consequences within.

Our mindset through and in response to tragedy, then, can make or break us. The issue is whether our thinking is regressive and circular, or linear. Whereas linear reasoning is directional and creative, regressive and circular reasoning turns in on itself, mulling over unproductive questions about what could or should or might have been. Like water spiralling down a drain, it sucks the brain into a sloth of self-pity. We pour much needed energy into things that can't be changed. For example, after losing the life and possessions we loved, our goal had been to get back to where we were. As long as that was our objective, tension increased. In stores, we were unable to find exactly what we had lost. Our home would never be the same, and none other could replace it. No matter how hard we tried, there was no going back. It was only when we released the past and determined to build and enjoy a new and different future that the capacity returned to enjoy the remaining benefits of our present and to anticipate improvement in the future.

We either let go of the past or we bind ourselves irretrievably to it. Like others on the hill, we didn't like the past when we went through it; we have no desire to continue living it in our minds. Stand firm, therefore, in the treasure of what you have left in the present, rather than being entangled by memories of what you lost in the past.

LOOK FOR A BENEFIT

No matter what we go through, as long as we are able to hold on to hope, the human spirit can prevail, but the loss of hope robs us of reason for living in the present and drive for striving for the future. Though it's normal to wrestle with God through our troubles, we need to be patient and remain true to our character. It is often during times of frailty that God releases His greatest blessings. Though our castles may fall in heaps of dust, God is able to transform our tears into rainbows of hope.

In our case, the explosion not only blew apart our home, it also blew apart some cages we had built for ourselves. Cages with bars we liked because they made us feel comfortable and secure. The blast tore them all away releasing us to pursue new and challenging ventures we probably would have never considered prior to the loss. Perhaps this is what Walt Disney meant when, from experience, he said that everyone should go bankrupt early in his career because of all that experience teaches. We should never allow tragedy to blind us to opportunities it might contain, however well camouflaged. With the proper positive perseverance, crisis that opens our minds to change may prove to be a gift.

HAVE WE HEALED?

The question has been asked, how much better would we have

coped if the insurance company had supported our claims rather than seeking to thwart them. Without doubt, much better! If our insurance company had stepped in with compassionate care, our whole family, which is normally very resilient, would have healed rapidly from its loss. Gratitude alone for insurance company kindness would have helped catapult us beyond the tragedy.

Have we healed? Have I healed? It's sometimes hard to know. What I have learned is that healing sometimes does not mean returning to the state you were before. The explosion in Port Hope, November 10, 1993, set in motion a sequence of events from which there is no return. In fact, one of the surest ways of insuring we will never heal is to set as our goal a return to what existed prior to the explosion. We cannot go back. We cannot recreate the past, however rosy hued it is in our memory. We can only go forward into our uncertain future, to build the best life we can, taking with us as much of the good, and asking God to release us from weights that would drag us down.

Are we healed? — Partially. Are we healing? — Certainly. Is there hope? — Definitely, wherever the human spirit refuses to fold in the presence of life's blasts.

> *One ship sails east*
> *And another sails west*
> *With the very same winds that blow, —*
> *'Tis the set of the sails*
> *And not the gales*
> *That tells the ship how to go.*
>
> —Anon

POSTSCRIPT

Two years after the explosion, 30 Ravine Drive has been sold to a construction company who repaired it to their own specifications for resale.

Andrea has many treasured friends in Oshawa and in Hamilton where she studies humanities at McMaster University. She earned four awards in her OAC year, including Ontario Scholar.

Jeremy has become a partner and Vice President in Master Creations Incorporated, a new software development firm. Educationally, he continues taking courses toward his Bachelor of Mathematics degree from the University of Waterloo.

My wife, Diane, continues as the sweet stabilizer of our home and is presently teaching in a temporary position for the Northumberland-Clarington Board of Education.

I am enjoying ministry among a happy and loving congregation at Harmony Road Baptist Church, Oshawa. Our biggest concern is how to handle the burgeoning growth our church is experiencing. I am also polishing a manual to assist in the management of insurance claims, entitled, *What The Insurance Company Will Not Tell You About Settling Your Claim.*

Our saga with the insurance company continues. Through pressure from our lawyer, the insurance company has now agreed to pay the Appraisal Award and a small portion of our legal expenses. Since we already paid thousands out of our own pocket for a public adjuster to manage the claim and bring the matter to Appraisal, our lawyer agrees that we should not be held responsible for any legal fees required to enforce the Appraisal decision. Since the company remains intractable to the end, the matter will have to be resolved before a judge.

CREDITS

PICTURES AND ILLUSTRATIONS

Order Form

Ordered By: (please print)

Name: _____

Address: _____

City: _____ Prov.: _____

Postal Code: _____ Telephone: _____

Please rush me additional copies:

Qty.	Title	Unit Price	Total
_____	*And the Pink Snow Fell*	$14.95	$_____
	Shipping ($2.00 first book - $1.00 each add. book):		$_____
	G.S.T. @ 7%:		$_____
	Total:		**$_____**

Payable by Cheque, Money Order or **VISA**

VISA #:_____ Expiry:_____

Signature:_____

**To order by phone, call our toll-free number,
1-800-238-6376
and have your credit card handy.**